BEST KNOWING JOY

BEYOND TRUST TO TRUTH

LOU POTEMPA
AUTHOR

AuthorHouse™
1663 Liberty Drive
Bloomington, IN 47403
www.authorhouse.com
Phone: 1-800-839-8640

Published by AuthorHouse 05/21/2014

ISBN: 978-1-4969-0500-0 (sc)
ISBN: 978-1-4969-0501-7 (e)

Library of Congress Control Number: 2014907261

authorHOUSE®

BEST KNOWING JOY

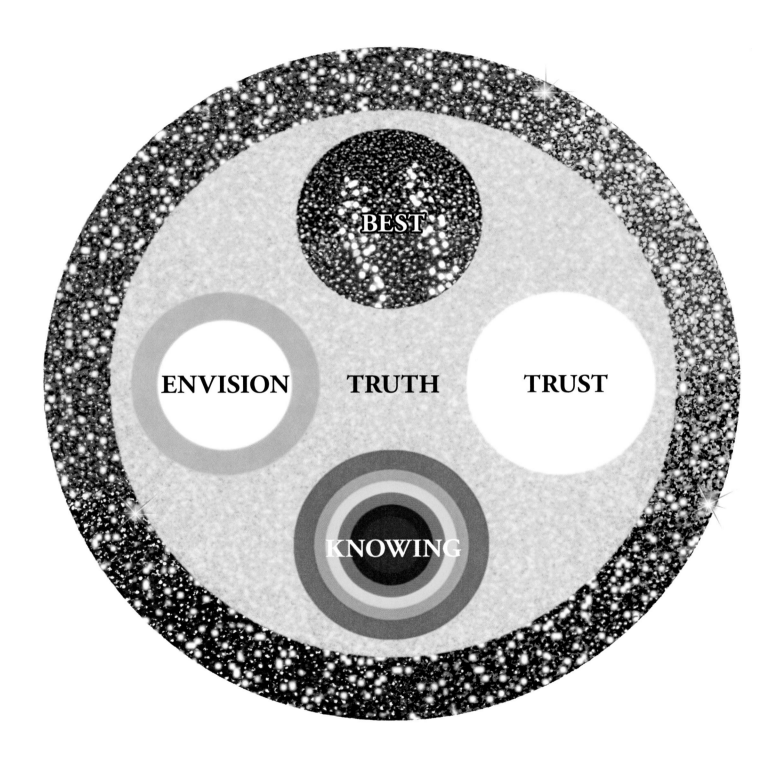

Contents

MANIFEST

AUTHOR'S COMMENT

'BEST KNOWING JOY' has been written to significantly change the world for the BEST. The approach is to provide a simplified understanding of the human experience in the evolution of the Universe and then empowering readers to realize what can be accomplished through use of the legacies we have inherited.

Through the decision to use and the use of our consciousness we can control TIME and thereby eliminate negative factors in our lives and bring about desirable outcomes through successive stages of cascading improved empowerment.

The 'BEST KNOWING JOY' process permits the over-coming of factors, some virtually insurmountable, and progressing in our lives to realize TRUTH and PURPOSE. Through the elevation and expansion of consciousness we become enabled to realize POTENTIAL, MANIFEST goals and experience JOY individually and collectively.

Merely scanning 'BEST KNOWING JOY' will change one's life.

Reading 'BEST KNOWING JOY' changes one's life for the best.

Universal application of the 'BEST KNOWING JOY' process will significantly change the world for the best.

FOREWARD

'BEST KNOWING JOY' is a guide to a process of empowerment, purpose and truth which will result in the achievement of desired outcomes. The book presents a challenging way to understand and engage in the events, relationships and consequential experiences of our lives. The approach is to convey a profound instruction in as simple and condensed manner as possible to reach and impact the largest readership possible. The intent is to describe a path to truth by which all people of all persuasions can attain the highest level of their potential.

The view taken is that we are no less than huge beneficiaries of the 13.7 billion years of evolution having occurred in the Universe. Sharing the human experience we are all endowed with legacies of LIGHT and TRUTH through which we have consciousness, advanced intelligence, self- awareness and free will providing the potential for vastly increased empowerment.

The 'BEST KNOWING JOY' process increases empowerment through the insightful recognition of factors related to the focus of human consciousness. Having once initially completing the entire process a person will have experienced a life change which will induce the desire to thoroughly integrate the process into the conduct of daily activities. The insights and perspective to be gained are so powerful that merely reading 'BEST KNOWING JOY' will make a difference in one's life.

The focus of consciousness is the key to successfully absorbing the process. The approach taken uses a combination that applies visual, audio and experiential senses in a precise manner allowing for application by a readership having a wide range of learning skills. In particular symbols, symbol protocols and graphic text symbol charts are used and are meant to be useful takeaways facilitating the ability to practice the process.

The final section of the book includes a matrix of strategies related to the specific application of the five stages of the process. This takeaway is presented in a general but most highly precise manner to enable practice and application by all people, everywhere and of every ability. The over-arching thought is that all have a birthright entitling them to be their BEST having KNOWING and realizing JOY. Successful realization of that achievement will result in a difference of magnitude in the human experience.

PRELUDE

THE HUGE HAPPENING

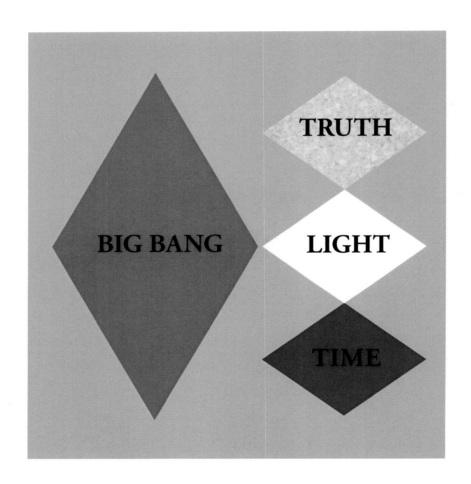

INTRODUCTION

'BEST KNOWING JOY' has been written to share the thought that we human beings have inherited the ability to successfully experience PURPOSE and TRUTH in our lives. To understand this presumptuous statement we must start our journey at the beginning which to the best of our present understanding is at the BIG BANG.

In the beginning....the BIG BANG will be described as having three Universal fundamental aspects, namely, TRUTH, LIGHT and TIME from which our birthrights arise.

TRUTH consists of the total reality of all facts and factors known, unknown, knowable and unknowable regarding LIGHT and TIME.

LIGHT is the totality of all facts and factors regarding space and the energy, matter and forces of the Universe.

TIME is a framework with which to describe, account for and relate the existence and emergence of TRUTH and LIGHT.

All that has ever transpired in the Universe in terms of our 'BEST KNOWING JOY' journey will be thought to be in accordance with TRUTH, LIGHT and TIME.

CONSCIOUSNESS LEVELS

LEVEL	*STAGE*	*ACTIVITY*
LEGACY	*DECISION*	*EXERCISE FREE WILL*
THRESHOLD	*TRUST*	*CONTROL TIME*
EMPOWERMENT		*IMPACT CONSCIOUSNESS*
	KNOWING	
	VISION	
	PURPOSE	
MANIFEST	*TRUTH*	*MANIFEST WILL*

CONSCIOUSNESS FOCUS LEVELS

As stated in the Introduction there are legacies related to TRUTH, LIGHT and TIME which prospectively endow us with the ability to experience significant attainment and accomplishment in our lives. In order that the reader understand from the outset the manner by which this is to be accomplished, the following is a summary description of how the legacies and consciousness will be merged.

In 'BEST KNOWING JOY' a process involving four levels of consciousness is developed, namely, LEGACY, THRESHOLD, EMPOWERMENT and MANIFEST. Therein six successive stages result in both the elevation and extension of consciousness.

LEGACY ....Exercise of Free Will results in a decision to acknowledge, accept and embrace our consciousness and the legacies related to the Universal fundamentals.

THRESHOLD.....TRUST is established through control of TIME and the consequent freeing of consciousness from negative burdens and impediments.

EMPOWERMENT.....A three stage process which elevates and extends consciousness leading to realization of POTENTIAL.

> KNOWING results when consciousness is focused on the LIGHT legacy and attendant TRUTH increasing empowerment. Other-consciousness results having enhanced awareness and understanding.

> VISION driven by Other-consciousness and TRUTH results in envisioning PURPOSE, Will and Sharing with Others. The clear sighted focus is directed to desired outcomes.

> PURPOSE is focused both individually and collectively on realizing the greatest POTENTIAL applied to pursuit of envisioned objectives.

MANIFEST.....An achievement level where TRUTH is the causative stage in the application of empowerment resulting in desired outcome realization and the experience of JOY.

As an additional aid and guide in absorbing and practicing the 'BEST KNOWING JOY' process at the conclusion of this PRELUDE section a page entitled Journey of Empowerment concisely summarizes the eight steps of empowerment related to the Consciousness Focus Levels.

LEGACY

COSMOS/LIFE ON EARTH

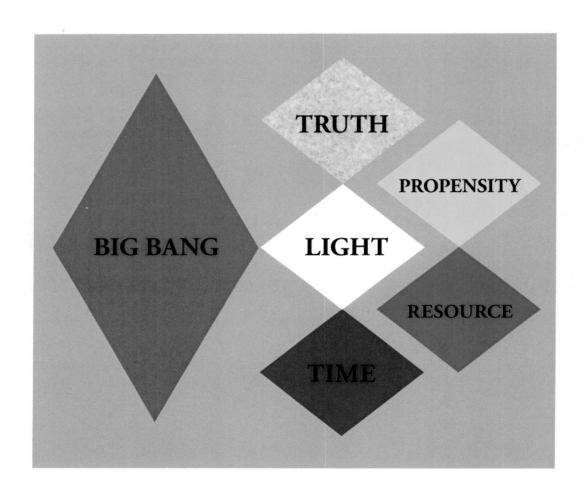

THE COSMOS/LIFE ON EARTH

Knowing that everything in the Universe can be traced back to the Big Bang, it seems reasonable to establish a context for our journey starting with several salient factors related to The Cosmos and Life on Earth. The Cosmos was created 13.7 billion years ago and can obviously, but all be it, thoroughly inadequately described as awesome.

Billions of galaxies containing billions of stars, black holes, planets, asteroids, sub-atomic particles, gravitational forces and many other known and unknown entities exist at levels staggering the imagination. Scientists amazingly have made great strides in discovering and understanding phenomena and features dating back more than 13 billion years. The science has indeed been established defining many laws and mechanisms by which creation has progressed starting with the Huge Happening when the first photon escaped the primordial plasma.

Planet Earth formed about 4.5 billion years ago and Life on Earth in the form of single cells appeared about 1 billion years later. The following 3 billion years consisted primarily of single cell and microorganism existence. Scientists have insightfully developed knowledge about these life forms as well as the progression and developments involving the evolution of insects, fish, reptiles and mammals through the unlocking of the mysteries of natural selection and the genetic code.

For the purpose of our 'BEST KNOWING JOY' journey this over simplified view regarding The Cosmos and Life On Earth is sufficient in that it is abundantly apparent that present day scientific knowledge gives us a highly credible basis for intelligently relating to the countless diverse aspects of the Universe. Having established this our interest lies in focusing on the most basic of the Universe's fundamental aspects.

Everything that has transpired in the Universe can be thought to be in accordance with TRUTH, LIGHT and TIME. To further advance this concept, LIGHT is seen as having two predominant over-arching characteristics, namely, PROPENSITY and RESOURCE. PROPENSITY is a generalized term relating to tendencies arising from the identity of entities in the realm of the Cosmos. RESOURCE is likewise related to the physicality and potential of the entities. The resulting template, as shown in the chart, broadly hints at a trajectory moving from the Huge Happening along a pathway of LIGHT and TRUTH legacies leading to Life on Earth preceeding the advent of human life forms.

HUMANITY

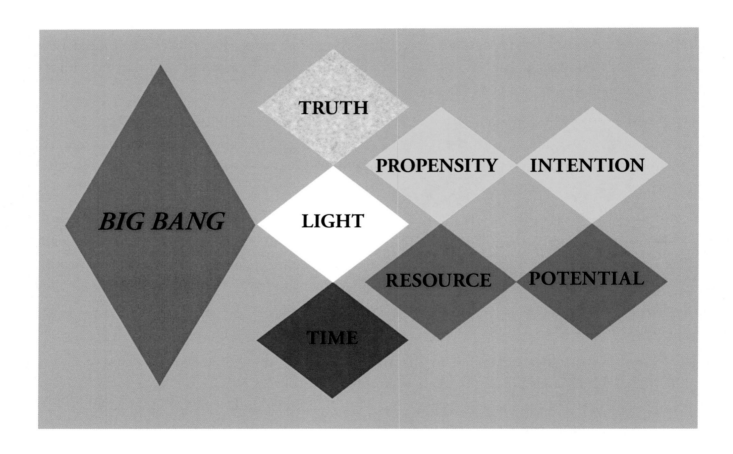

HUMANITY

All that has transpired and emerged from the instant of the Huge Happening can reasonably be viewed as occurring for the benefit of Humanity. Obviously, the emergence of the planet Earth 4.5 billion years ago is consistent with that view. The history of the evolution of life forms on planet Earth emerging from scientific study provides a base of knowledge regarding the progression of human development.

Evolution leading to Humanity began approximately 3.5 billion years ago. The family tree of Humanity becomes more definitive when the branches leading to the advent of Neanderthal and other ancestral species diverged about 500 thousand years ago. Interestingly, the era called that of the "fully modern human beings" did not begin until about 50 thousand years ago. In the context of our journey and the manner in which TIME is to be dealt with these time periods are in a way somewhat incomprehensible.

During the latter period human consciousness markedly increased to the highest level on Earth and, to the best of our present knowledge, unique in the Universe. The advances of the past 6 thousand years and, in particular, those in more recent time, present significant evidence of the emergence and impact of increased human consciousness on Life on planet Earth.

As consciousness is seen to develop it becomes more appropriate when referring to the pathway of human development to use the terms INTENTION and POTENTIAL to replace the PROPENSITY and RESOURCE terminology still applicable to the remainder of the Cosmos. INTENTION becomes a dominant factor with increasing human consciousness. POTENTIAL influenced by genetic developments as well as consciousness, expands and is realized in response to ever increasingly developed INTENTION.

The emerging INTENTION and POTENTIAL along with the expansion of knowledge and increased application of skills and capabilities led to asignificantly advanced Humanity level, namely, the Human Experience.

HUMAN EXPERIENCE

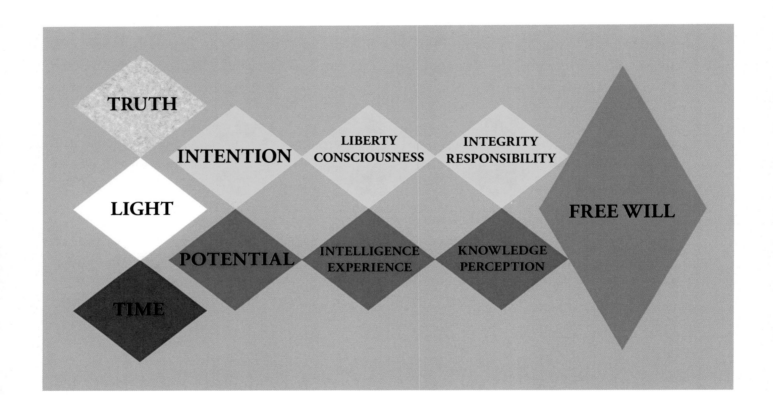

HUMAN EXPERIENCE

Those living the Human Experience to the best of our knowledge are the most advanced species in the entire Cosmos. A path tracing our human evolution from the Huge Happening through to the present day influence of the LIGHT and TRUTH legacies can be seen in the development of traits emanating from emerging and developing INTENTION and POTENTIAL.

INTENTION emerges as the consciousness of beings rises over the centuries. Liberty, the ability of make voluntary choice, is increasingly realized as life beyond mere survival arises due to increased mental abilities and skills. Responsibility, being accountable, increases with more interaction and dependence among beings. Integrity becomes an increasingly complex and highly valued trait as the Human Experience continues.

POTENTIAL with its extent always unknown has as its basis native physicality and intelligence. Experience as a circumstance of life is always demonstrable and influential relative to POTENTIAL. Likewise, knowledge has always been a major contributing element in both the capacity and realization of POTENTIAL. Self-awareness to a high degree distinguishes humans to an incomparable degree among all life species on planet Earth. Perception, influenced by self-awareness, with its interaction with personal ego is the most common and private of the traits relating to attitude and performance in life. Importantly, creativity and negativity are two opposite poles in the range of factors impacting exercise and realization of POTENTIAL.

Inherent intelligence and life experiences can create a minimal basis for the selection of individual INTENTION. Significantly, with increasing knowledge and perception gained through meaningful realization of POTENTIAL, INTENTION can be elevated resulting in the decision to conduct our lives with a sense of responsibility and integrity. Of great importance, the meaningful exercise of FREE WILL can be achieved with the proper cultivation of the Human Experience. Free Will, indeed unique to the Human Experience, enables the choice and focus of our Will in pursuit of empowerment and PURPOSE.

FREE WILL

FREE WILL

Free Will unique to the Human Experience is a power of self-determination. When exercised with knowledge, responsibility and integrity this power enables the focus and choice of our individual Will. Free Will conceptually has extensive latitude ranging from 1) the meaning of life, the attainment of wisdom and the understanding of being to 2) the creation and exercise of power in its many forms. Free Will enables a decision to pursue and access elevated consciousness. The recognition and exercise of Free Will are very important factors to the quality of one's life and are necessary and critical to engaging in the 'BEST KNOWING JOY' process.

The exercise of Free Will is accomplished through focus of consciousness. Communicating with consciousness is readily accomplished through a process of simple decision making and use of an easily visualized symbol. The first step is a selection between the concepts of LIGHT and darkness. The decision for LIGHT is to be made for several reasons. LIGHT is required for sight. Darkness symbolically conveys lack of sight and negativity. Secondly, LIGHT as heretofore defined is one of the fundamental aspects of the Universe and therefore a major factor in the 'BEST KNOWING JOY' process. Third, the LIGHT legacy related to the Human Experience is an important factor in our journey.

In order to focus consciousness and exercise Free Will, choose LIGHT with its three functionalities by momentarily visualizing a bright white LIGHT in your consciousness. Through the process of mentally switching on LIGHT the darkness and all it relates to in your consciousness is rejected and instantly released. This simple focused action and imagery involving FREE WILL is an important and powerful first step in the TRUST stage of the 'BEST KNOWING JOY' process to be discussed further in the following TRUST section..

JOURNEY OF EMPOWERMENT

The PRELUDE of our JOURNEY OF EMPOWERMENT has been completed with the rejection of darkness through the focus of consciousness and the exercise of Free Will. This is the first of eight steps as shown below in what will be experienced by the reader as a remarkable cascading of personal empowerment.

FREE WILL	REJECT DARKNESS	EMPOWERING LIGHT
LIGHT	REJECT NEGATIVITY	EMPOWERING INSTANT (DISOWN TIME PAST)
INSTANT	ACCEPT REALITY	EMPOWERING TRUST
TRUST	FOCUS CONSCIOUSNESS	EMPOWERING KNOWING
KNOWING	REJECT DISTRACTION	EMPOWERING VISION (DISOWN FEAR, GREED)
VISION	ENVISION DESIRE	EMPOWERING PURPOSE
PURPOSE	GIVE BEST	EMPOWERING TRUTH
TRUTH	GIVE MANIFEST	GAIN REALIZATION, JOY

As shown above each step involves a decision, action or realization which results in empowerment for a subsequent stage, ultimately giving rise to the attainment of the MANIFEST level. The details leading to the understanding, practice and application of the stages follow in the PROCESS and PROTOCOL sections.

PROCESS

THRESHOLD

TRUST

EMPOWERMENT

KNOWING

VISION

PURPOSE

MANIFEST

TRUTH

TRUST

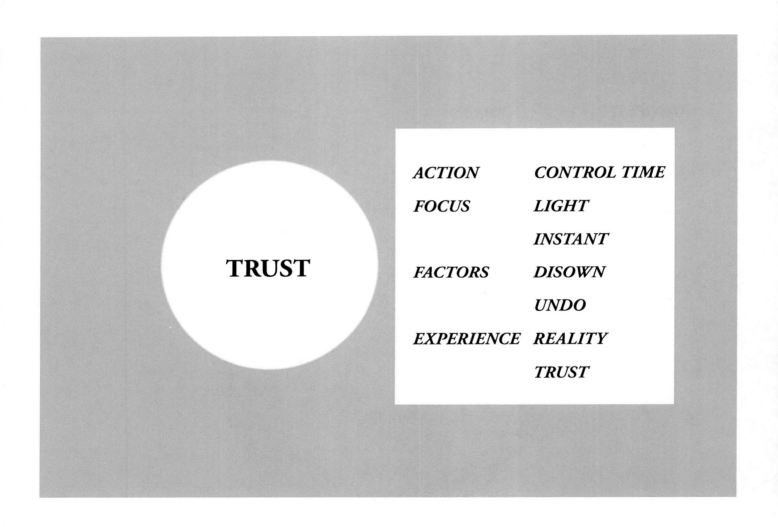

TRUST

In exercising Free Will and choosing LIGHT in the prior section, we instantly focused our consciousness on LIGHT and simultaneously released darkness. This is significant in that it is necessary for advancement of our power of consciousness that we deal with our personal darkness, namely, the psychological "baggage" which distracts or impedes us from the highest, most effective use of our INTENTION and POTENTIAL in pursuit of PURPOSE.

The "baggage" which we all have to a greater or lesser extent exists in two forms. The first is the accumulation of regrets, prohibitions and mental blocks that arise from personal shortcomings, mistakes, prejudices, addictions and sensitivities. The second form is the array of roadblocks, envy, intimidation and presumed inadequacies that result from competition, conflicts and assorted adverse interactions with other people. The lives of individuals, the fortunes of societies, the fate of nations and, indeed, the course of world history have experienced limitation, suffered great frustration and momentous tragedies arising from the darkness of negativity.

Negativity exists in consciousness as recollections of episodes in Past Time. Past Time can be thought of as a repository of these recollections which impact us in the present but in reality are over and done with. Effectively shedding darkness is a major personal challenge. Attempting to merely overlook negativity is not an effective way to deal with Past Time. Thinking back to the earlier LIGHT/darkness choice, however, suggests a path to a powerful, breakthrough solution.

If we focus our Free Will on disowning the personal darkness and undoing the negativity related to others in the present INSTANT of TIME, we will have directed our consciousness to where reality and TRUTH exist without the attendant burden of memory. Past Time thereby has no root in INSTANT where only reality and TRUTH exist. By the Free Will choice of INSTANT we have effectively instantaneously controlled TIME. Doing so simultaneously with and in the context of our earlier LIGHT/darkness choice, we switch on INSTANT and abolish the darkness of Past Time. The result is that LIGHT has been switched on in a consciousness free of "baggage". This is an extremely significant achievement.

Recognize that LIGHT, INSTANT, reality and TRUTH give rise to TRUST which is a threshold to the future. TRUST over fear is an enduring not fleeting trait which definitively projects into the future. TRUST and TRUTH therefore establish a requisite dimension of TIME extending INSTANT to become a substantive base from which our journey will continue. More discussion of TRUST is included in the TRUST SYMBOL PROTOCOL section.

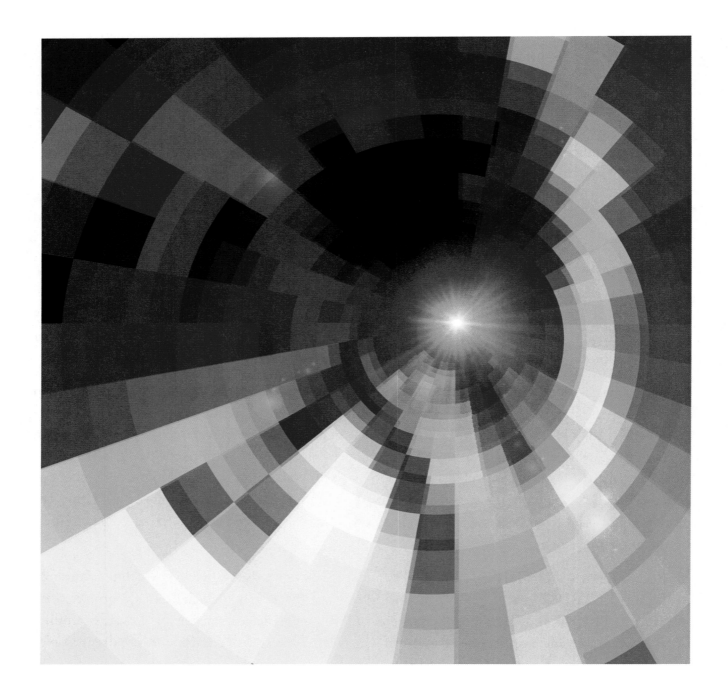

EMPOWERMENT

KNOWING

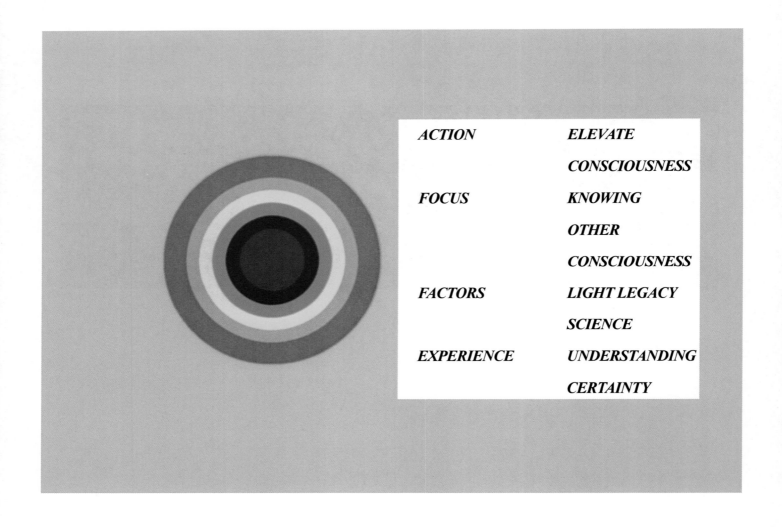

ACTION	*ELEVATE*
	CONSCIOUSNESS
FOCUS	*KNOWING*
	OTHER
	CONSCIOUSNESS
FACTORS	*LIGHT LEGACY*
	SCIENCE
EXPERIENCE	*UNDERSTANDING*
	CERTAINTY

KNOWING

KNOWING is the possession of the Universally known, knowable and unknowable through unique human powers of consciousness and awareness. In the context of 'BEST KNOWING JOY' the term KNOWING is related to LIGHT and TRUTH which are both fundamental aspects of the Universe. LIGHT encompasses all elements of energy, space, matter and derivatives thereof existing in the Universe. TRUTH is the omnipresent, changeless and empowering reality of the Universe.

Empowerment derives from KNOWING as a result of insightful recognition, understanding and application of the facts relating to LIGHT and TRUTH at one or more of three levels of consciousness. The levels being sub-consciousness defined as a phenomena of mental life by which many automatic processes involving mind and body are controlled. Consciousness is a level commonly defined as the state of being conscious with power of self-knowledge, knowledge, internal perception and awareness of sensation. The third level is referred to as Other-consciousness. This level results from the elevation and expansion of consciousness due to the extension of understanding, awareness and activity related to the LIGHT and TRUTH legacies..

TRUST and a high degree of certainty exist regarding the KNOWING stage due to the extensive base of scientific knowledge relating to the multitude of diverse factors associated with LIGHT and TRUTH.

LIGHT LEGACY

HIGGS BOSONS	DARK ENERGY	VISION
LEPTONS	ELEMENTS	HUMANS
FORCES	SOLAR SYSTEM	ANIMALS
PROTONS	GALAXIES	PLANTS
MICROWAVES	STARS	INSECTS
PHOTONS	HYDROGEN	CELL LIFE
	LIGHT	

KNOWING

KNOWING about LIGHT and TRUTH is to have a measure of knowledge about a truly immense and astonishing evolution. The creation of a Universe composed of billions of galaxies and stars over a period of 13.7 billion years has also resulted in the origin of life and an evolution from single cell entities to those of us sharing the Human Experience. The facts indeed stagger the imagination.

It is significant that through the application of the human mind scientific discoveries have resulted in an understanding of many of the fundamental truths and laws of the Universe. These extend from identification of ultra-diminutive species of particles present at the Huge Happening to the genetic code governing all of life and, beyond, to the conception and development of two vastly different sets of theories describing the basics of matter and the forces of nature.

The evolution of LIGHT originating with the first photon emerging at the Huge Happening can be traced and understood in terms of scientific knowledge extending through to our present Human Experience. The evolution, in vastly over simplified terms, can therefore be depicted clearly showing a connection between all things in the Universe as everything ultimately has their origination in LIGHT. The rationale for LIGHT as a basis for KNOWING as well as the underlying LIGHT legacy accruing to the Human Experience is evident.

It is important to understand that the science related to all aspects of the Cosmos and Life extending to the Human Experience although extensive is obviously far from being complete and today is confronted with challenging unknowns. KNOWING encompasses, however, the yet incomplete understanding of such matters as the existence of the Higgs boson and Dark Energy as well as quantum factors related to human VISION.

ELEVATED CONSCIOUSNESS

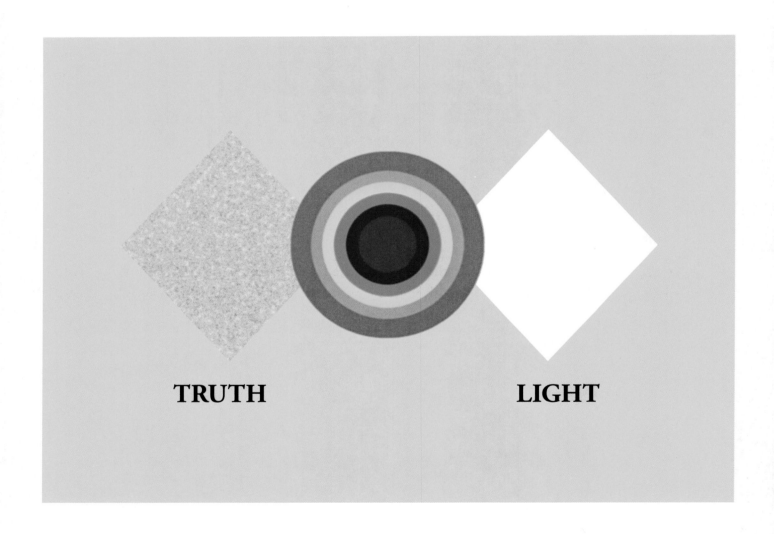

TRUTH   **LIGHT**

KNOWING

The empowerment derived from KNOWING results from understanding to a required level of specificity facts and factors concerning the LIGHT and TRUTH legacies. Other-consciousness is thereby given awareness, insight and empowerment in receiving a recognition and understanding regarding pursuit of desired outcomes involving matters related to LIGHT and TRUTH legacies. A directed focus of Other-consciousness which is informed and constructive relative to desired outcomes is described in detail in the Symbol Protocol section..

In addition to KNOWING conveying understanding and empowerment to subsequent stages of the 'BEST KNOWING JOY' process there are five notable activities where KNOWING is operative:

First, awareness of the TRUTH related to the reality of matters under Instant consideration.

Second, the prospective reality of outcomes related to Will and desires.

Third, manifestation of unforeseen events and entities related to pursued outcomes.

Fourth, human reactions and occurrences which are unpredicted or otherwise unknowable.

Fifth, awareness and influence resulting from empowerment given and shared by Others.

As the first stage at the EMPOWERMENT level, KNOWING advancing from the TRUST stage creates a solid base from which empowerment cascades to the VISION and PURPOSE stages. Very importantly, TRUST carried forward and combined with the influence of KNOWING empowering Other-consciousness are necessary factors to the action of TRUTH as a definitive causative factor.

VISION

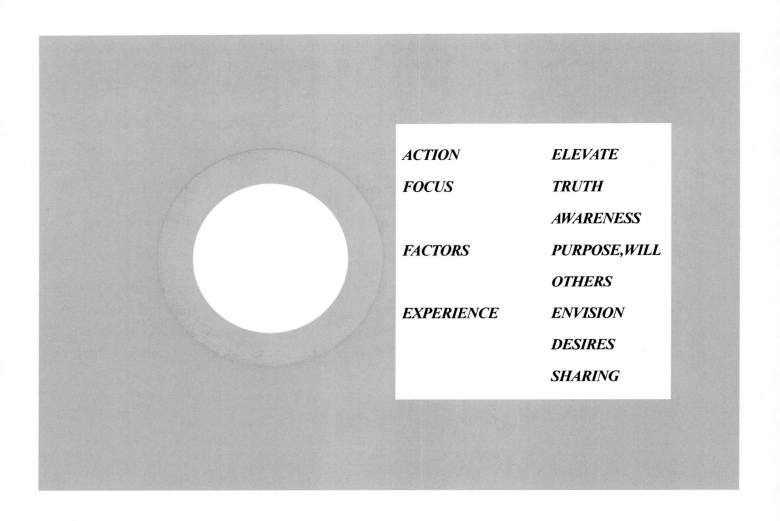

ACTION   ELEVATE

FOCUS   TRUTH

                         AWARENESS

FACTORS   PURPOSE,WILL

                         OTHERS

EXPERIENCE   ENVISION

                         DESIRES

                         SHARING

VISION

VISION is the stage where consciousness has been elevated through KNOWING empowered by the LIGHT and TRUTH legacies and extended to the level of Other-consciousness. The VISION stage enables the ability to envision, that is, view clearly our desires and Will in the extended Instant where TRUTH prevails and emotional distractions are disowned. Other-consciousness existing in VISION provides awareness and sensitivity to factors both understood and beyond immediate cognition. Ego, perception and ignorance are discredited in the context of the cascading empowerment as fears, anger and pride are disowned.

VISION is the creative stage of the EMPOWERMENT level where the envisioning establishes specific expectations and envisioning relative to the desires, Will and Others. As these factors are decided upon and appropriate symbols, chosen, consciousness is focused on targeted outcomes. Once initiated our consciousness in each case continuously maintains an intensive awareness and focus on developments and responses. Activities envisioned and initiated in VISION are generally advanced by means of the PURPOSE stage and consummated in the TRUTH stage of the MANIFEST level.

The cascading within the EMPOWERMENT level is given impetus through both the focus of VISION relative to personal goals and the empowerment shared with and contributed by Others. The recognition of the importance of and dependence on the contribution of Others requires ongoing attention to both our joint activity with and well being of Others.. The importance of this aspect of VISION cannot be over emphasized.

The SYMBOL PROTOCOL section includes a discussion of procedures related to VISION..

PURPOSE

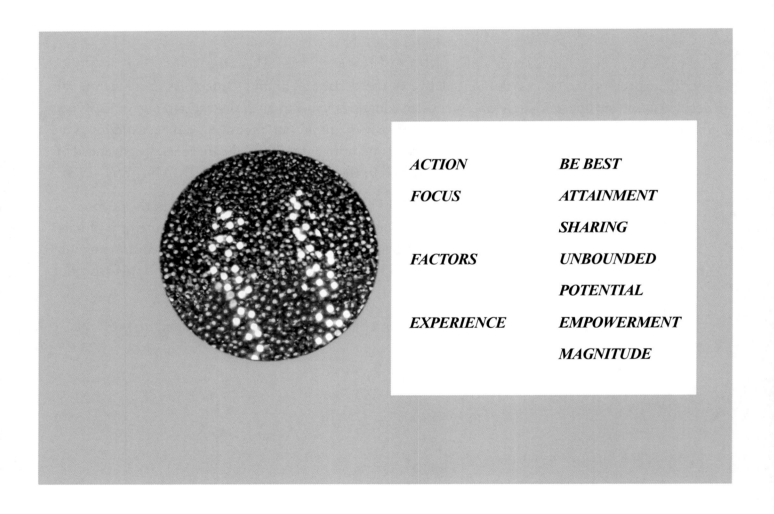

ACTION	*BE BEST*
FOCUS	*ATTAINMENT*
	SHARING
FACTORS	*UNBOUNDED*
	POTENTIAL
EXPERIENCE	*EMPOWERMENT*
	MAGNITUDE

PURPOSE

PURPOSE is the third stage in the EMPOWERMENT level of the 'BEST KNOWING JOY' process culminating the effort leading to the ultimate achievement of desired Will. The stage is an extremely important aspect of our state of Being as it is the means by which VISION is advanced towards realization. Recognizing the insights from the elevation of consciousness through KNOWING, the envisioning of Will during VISION and the awareness gained through Other-consciousness makes it evident that PURPOSE must necessarily be broad in scope involving both the INTENTION and POTENTIAL of our Being.

PURPOSE can be viewed and understood by simultaneously focusing consciousness on both the INTENTION and the POTENTIAL. Many aspects of INTENTION have already been considered at this juncture. In contrast, POTENTIAL in the context of cascading empowerment is unknown in extent but with regard to magnitude can reasonably be deemed to be unbounded. With that perspective and the INTENTION to have a PURPOSE of magnitude relative to all activities in every Instant, the following evolution of a statement of PURPOSE emerges:

INDIVIDUAL......BE the BEST that I am capable of being........which in
the instance of unbounded POTENTIAL can be restated as:

INDIVIDUAL......BE the BEST that I AM.......recognizing empowerment
as fully applied in any and all possible contexts.

A critical aspect of PURPOSE is the sharing of empowerment between the individual and Others in cooperative activities as well as in support of individual and collective general well-being. The resulting all inclusive statement of PURPOSE relative to efforts with Others is:

COLLECTIVE.....BE the BEST that WE ARE.

Recognizing the universal dependence of each of us on one another that exists to some extent in all situations, it is logical that the Collective statement of PURPOSE is relevant and applicable to everyone. The universally applicable statement therefore is:

BE THE BEST THAT WE ARE

As PURPOSE is applied, POTENTIAL magnitude in support of INTENTION is given due attention as empowerment is advanced to the MANIFEST level. See the SYMBOL PROTOCOL for additional information and guidance.

MANIFEST

TRUTH

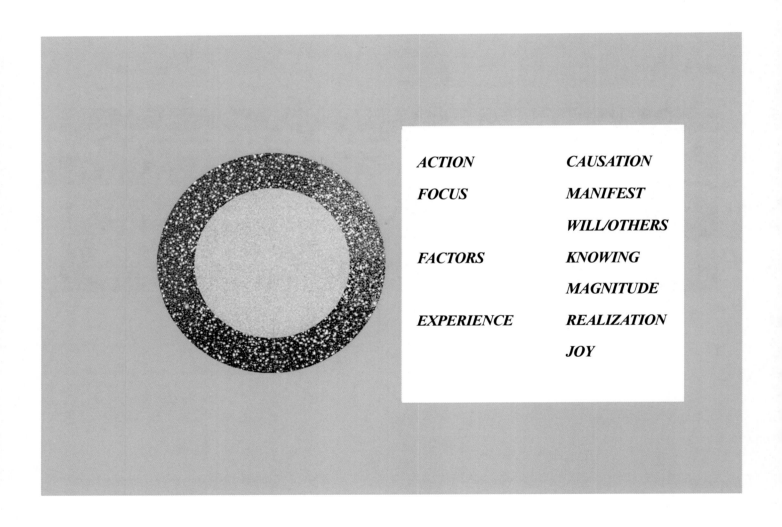

ACTION　　　*CAUSATION*

FOCUS　　　*MANIFEST*

　　　　　WILL/OTHERS

FACTORS　　*KNOWING*

　　　　　MAGNITUDE

EXPERIENCE　*REALIZATION*

　　　　　JOY

TRUTH

The 'BEST KNOWING JOY' process progressing through the EMPOWERMENT level advances to the MANIFEST level where the outcomes being caused through the action of consciousness are realized and observed. TRUTH is the causation stage at the MANIFEST level. It is the stage where Will and desire from VISION, and POTENTIAL and magnitude from PURPOSE converge in advance of causation. Causation then occurring through KNOWING and the focus of Other-Consciousness results in the personal experience of the realization of Will and the MANIFEST benefit to Others.

There are three broad categories in the stage which share the common attribute that TRUTH realized through KNOWING by way of Other-consciousness is a significant contributing factor. The first causation category results as the individual directly experiences MANIFEST simply following after the PURPOSE stage. The second category requires extended intense focus of Other-consciousness to complete the envisioning process initiated in the VISION stage. Category three is where MANIFEST is realized as awareness and understanding of the unknown and unknowable are brought to Other-consciousness directly through the spontaneous effect of the LIGHT and TRUTH legacies.

TRUTH being a fundamental aspect of the Universe is an over-arching power critical to the life, freedom and JOY of the Human Experience. The pursuit and realization of TRUTH through practice and application of the 'BEST KNOWING JOY' process represents meritorious achievement in a life driven by PURPOSE. Completing the journey through the TRUTH stage underscores the two factors absolutely critical to the Human Experience both individually and collectively, namely, FREEDOM and JOY.

Guidance regarding the practice of MANIFEST and TRUTH is included in the SYMBOL PROTOCOL section.

PROGRESS AND BEYOND

The "BEST KNOWING JOY" journey having progressed from the Huge Happening through the MANIFEST level and TRUTH stage has provided information regarding the rationale for the process, a description of the stages, key points related to engaging consciousness to activate the stages and the identification of the results which will occur as the process advances. As an aid to assist the reader in absorbing, retaining and subsequently practicing and applying this information, summary charts and descriptive symbols have been used as supplements to the text.

Progressing through the Process section, some level of increased empowerment will undoubtedly have been realized by the reader if the focus of consciousness specified has been attained. An important element of achieving the focus and empowerment will have been the impact of the visualization of the five stage symbols. It is consequently likely that many readers at the current achievement level will be able to proceed to the MANIFEST section of the book and effectively practice the process as it appears in THE TEMPLATE prescription.

Everyone will gain the empowerment and realization from the process, however, directly in proportion to their ability to communicate with consciousness. The use of symbols has been purposely extensive and is extremely effective in that regard. The benefit to be gained by learning of the techniques discussed in the first pages entitled SYMBOLS in the following Protocol section will be significant. Applying the SYMBOLS techniques will greatly accelerate the entire familiarization process. Time spent becoming proficient with techniques which are simple but unlike any with which one may be familiar will be substantially rewarded in not only the successful application of the process but also in garnering the additional guidance and insights associated with the attendant stage symbol protocols..

PROTOCOL

SYMBOLS

STAGE SYMBOL PROTOCOL

TRUST

KNOWING

VISION

PURPOSE

TRUTH

SYMBOLS

'BEST KNOWING JOY' is about applying consciousness to achieve PURPOSE, TRUTH and JOY at highest levels of human POTENTIAL. Consciousness involving mind, body and emotions needs to be engaged, focused, empowered and causative to accomplish this ambitious objective. Visual symbols ascribed contextual and detailed meaning and significance have been used to facilitate rapid and penetrating communication and retention of information to all elements of consciousness. A description of the SYMBOLS representing the five stages and comments regarding the use of the SYMBOLS will make evident their value in the focus of consciousness.

WHITE LIGHT......Focus on unblemished LIGHT which represents a measure of TIME where the past is disowned and all manner of negativity released. Recognizing the uniqueness of the INSTANT we become aware of an experience of reality and TRUTH. We associate the experience with a feeling of TRUST supplanting anxiety and fear in our consciousness. The disc is entitled TRUST and symbolizes a THRESHOLD level. The WHITE LIGHT disc may also be used as a trigger for initiating transfer between stages throughout the process.

LIGHT SPECTRUM........The focus in the KNOWING stage is affected by visualizing with the mind's eye concentric rings of the LIGHT spectrum ranging from ultra-violet to infra-red. The rings represent a collective six levels of knowledge and consciousness. While focusing on the spectrum, attention is primarily directed to the LIGHT and TRUTH legacies and the related empowerment and awareness associated with consciousness elevation and expansion. The latter is identified as Other Consciousness.

LEGACY SPHERE...........The SYMBOL signifying the empowerment passing to the VISION stage is a circle having an inner LIGHT circle and a surrounding gold TRUTH ring. The SYMBOL is most appropriately visualized as a three dimensional sphere as the inner circle is a space where PURPOSE, Will and Other persons will be envisioned in relation to desired activities and outcomes. The outer TRUTH ring is the region from which the awareness and understanding associated with Other Consciousness and the empowerment contributed by Other persons are brought to the LIGHT sphere where envisioning will occur without distortion arising from adverse distractions.

HOLOGRAM.................The PURPOSE SYMBOL depicts the complex dimensionality of LIGHT and TRUTH as well as the total commitment of empowerment and inherent POTENTIAL by the focused practitioner. Focusing on PURPOSE, the last of the EMPOWERMENT level stages, through use of the replica relates the unlimited magnitude as well as the breadth and depth of POTENTIAL to the multitudinous points of the SYMBOL hologram. Likewise, the many aspects of EMPOWERMENT are dramatically and simultaneously brought to attention in stunning fashion by the instantaneous and boundless combinations of an actual hologram reacting to

SYMBOLS

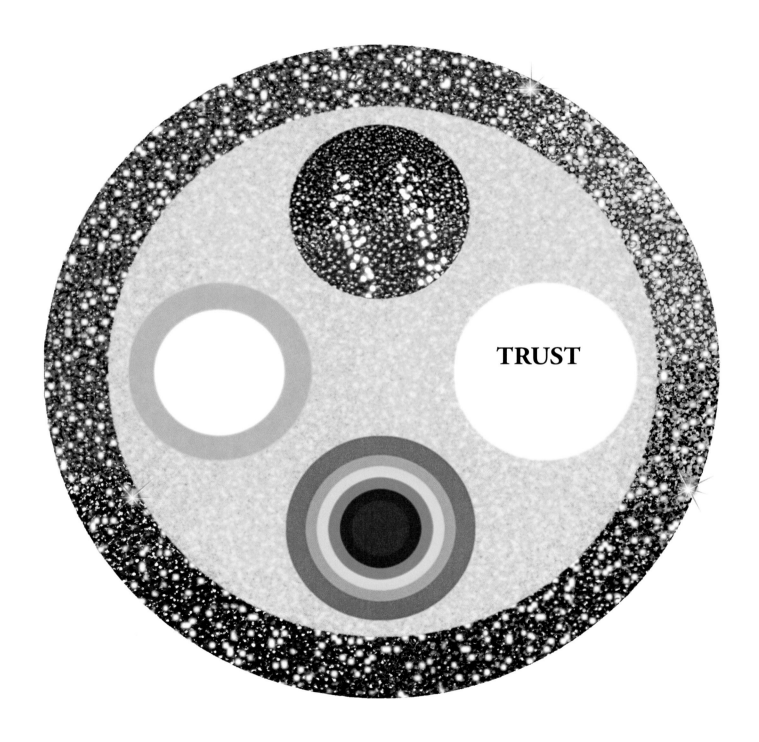

TRUST

varying LIGHT input. A 3 dimensional holographic visualization is an outstanding backdrop onto which the PURPOSE stage BEST statement is projected..

GOLDNESS.....................The culmination of the focused EMPOWERMENT effort in the final TRUTH stage is symbolized by the golden disc encircled by a holographic ring which recognizes attainment resulting from the preceding cascade of power. Manifesting results as KNOWING brings to causation all of the relevant factors at the TRUTH stage including the consummate human experience of JOY.

The usefulness and effectiveness of SYMBOLS is directly applicable to the five stages as described in the previous PROCESS section. Importantly, SYMBOLS will provide the vehicle for engaging in the comprehensive practice of the 'BEST KNOWING JOY' process when they are integrated into the STAGE SYMBOL PROTOCOLS. The command of large volumes of information, understanding and awareness accessed through the SYMBOLS and related visualization and envisioning sequences have been specifically and carefully integrated for each of the stages.

PROTOCOL

TRUST

TRUST SYMBOL PROTOCOL

The TRUST stage has been created beginning with the exercise of FREE WILL resulting in the outcome that LIGHT has been received in consciousness and darkness rejected. The decision has been made to definitively deal with negativity, that is, things in our past lives which are impediments to personal empowerment and achievement. Choosing LIGHT, a field of WHITE LIGHT is seen.

Choosing to identify the WHITE LIGHT with the present INSTANT of TIME, consciousness in a simple but effective way can be focused solely on the reality of the INSTANT. In the INSTANT, reality preempts memory and Past Time. In the reality of the INSTANT sense awareness that there is no use for or gain attendant with negativity. The WHITE LIGHT is seen as shining markedly brighter.

The reality of the INSTANT seen in the WHITE LIGHT is without exception always the TRUTH preempting fear. It can be said that TRUST in the TRUTH of the INSTANT exists if the fear of Past Time is absent and, further, if fear of the future can be dismissed. Recognizing the future is unknowable it is reasonable that any fear of the future can be dismissed in the INSTANT. Consequently, very importantly, INSTANT TRUST is justified. .

Recognizing that the INSTANT is always the first step into the future it is reasonable to confidently attribute to TRUST the measure of TIME greater than an INSTANT requisite to circumstances, an extended present period, be it minutes, hours or beyond. Consequently, through the TRUST stage, control of TIME can be effectively gained in matters of consciousness. This is an important insight.

A WHITE LIGHT disc accordingly symbolizes TRUST.

KNOWING

TRUST

KNOWING SYMBOL PROTOCOL

KNOWING is the stage where the LIGHT and TRUTH legacies are viewed in relation to human consciousness. Awareness and understanding derived from the two legacies are a source of significant empowerment of consciousness. Facilitating the focus of consciousness in the KNOWING stage is accomplished through use of a stage symbol featuring the visible LIGHT band color spectrum. The LIGHT SYMBOL is a circular disc composed of six spectrum colored concentric rings each ascribing either a level of consciousness or a degree of knowledge related to LIGHT and TRUTH.

The KNOWING SYMBOL may be viewed fully formed in its entirety while simultaneously effectively focusing consciousness on the LIGHT and TRUTH legacies. Alternatively, visualization may be used. This approach facilitates focus and takes advantage of the fact that use of disciplined eye motion patterns can positively affect communication within consciousness.

A first step in the alternate is to either 1) rotate closed eyes to trace images of concentric circles of the six colors one circle at a time or 2) visualize the colored circles forming the rings being consecutively positioned from an ultra-violet center to the infra-red outer ring. These steps are done using the white TRUST disc as a pallet on which to project shape, colors and motion.

A second step associates levels of knowledge with the levels of consciousness. The procedure consists of alternately prescribing specific levels of knowledge and of consciousness to the concentric rings again progressing from ultra-violet to infra-red. The individual elements of knowledge are known, knowable and KNOWING and of the latter are sub-consciousness, consciousness and Other-consciousness. The resultant labeling of known, sub-consciousness, knowable, consciousness, KNOWING, Other-consciousness sharpens the focus on the legacies and the empowerment of the KNOWING stage..

The KNOWING SYMBOL conveys the context and certainty of the empowerment arising in Other-consciousness from the gaining of awareness and understanding via the LIGHT and TRUTH legacies.

VISION

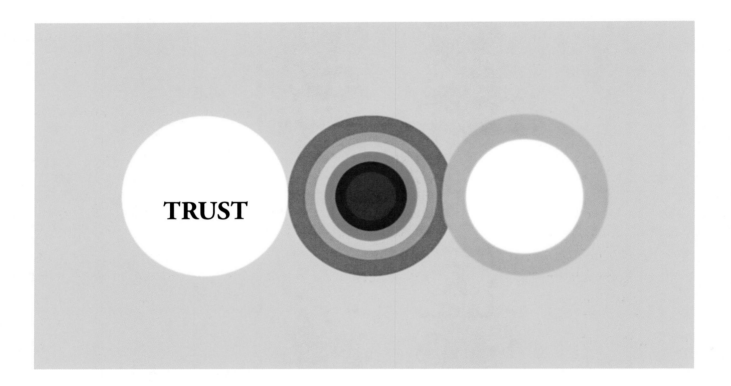

VISION SYMBOL PROTOCOL

The VISION SYMBOL emphasizes the focus of consciousness on the envisioning of all aspects of LIGHT and the over-arching power of TRUTH. The SYMBOL is a WHITE LIGHT disc encircled with the golden TRUTH ring. In order to emphasize the elevated empowerment at the VISION stage a third dimension may be added to the SYMBOL. In the mind's eye the SYMBOL would then be viewed as a LIGHT sphere encircled with a golden outer shell.

A first step associated with the VISION SYMBOL involves the golden outer shell engulfing and merging with the LIGHT sphere symbolizing displacing personal adversely distractive factors which may be present at the outset of the stage. These factors are of no constructive value and are therefore disowned. This action further represents TRUTH engulfing every aspect of the VISION stage whereby envisioning is enabled through the action of Other-consciousness.

As VISION is the stage where desire, Will and Others are to be envisioned, the VISION sphere displays a large window through which desired images surrounded and filled with WHITE LIGHT can be viewed. The envisioning is to be focused on not only the desired outcomes but also on the sharing of empowerment by all involved. Envisioning occurs at a level of detail or abstraction which may be enhanced through a tacit statement of the sought after outcome. This two-fold action is highly effective in the uncompromised truthfulness of the stage. VISION involving Others, it is to be noted, very importantly often entails the sharing of one's well being.

It is noted that whereas TRUST and KNOWING are stages to access and incrementally add to or gain empowerment through relatively brief occasional exercise, VISION is an on-going consciousness working stage. Highly focused consciousness at the VISION stage drives the empowerment that is critical to the subsequent PURPOSE stage and the MANIFEST level.

PURPOSE

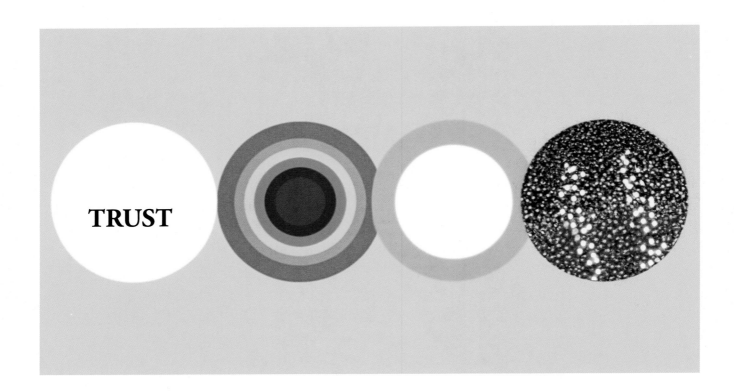

PURPOSE SYMBOL PROTOCOL

PURPOSE is the stage at which we express our INTENTION to best use our uncompromised inherent POTENTIAL to the maximum. Expressed in terms applicable to unbounded POTENTIAL and the range of possible diverse Willed outcomes, our PURPOSE is stated as ***BE THE BEST THAT WE ARE.***

In PURPOSE we are empowered to pursue and share with Others activities that have been envisioned in the VISION stage. The empowerment is activated through the focus of our consciousness on the attainment of objectives related to the variety of Willed and desired outcomes. The resulting activities derive from both the directed application of individual POTENTIAL and, importantly, the contribution and empowerment shared by Others.

The PURPOSE SYMBOL simply replicates an image of components of the LIGHT spectrum. The SYMBOL represents elevated consciousness focused on the many specifics envisioned in the VISION stage being enhanced through the empowerment of the PURPOSE stage.

The SYMBOL is a 2 dimensional depiction of a 3D holographic image where light can be scattered, directed and viewed at various angles and spectral frequencies. It is a representation of the envisioning, empowerment and attainment at the PURPOSE stage. A more dynamic alternate three dimensional method to focus PURPOSE consciousness can be achieved through the visualizing of a vertically rotating LIGHT spectrum sphere. The sphere is constructed with an ultra-violet sphere center onto which five successive spherical spectrum colored layers are laminated.

The PURPOSE SYMBOL in either configuration is used to provide the space on which the statement ***BE THE BEST THAT WE ARE*** is to be envisioned. The statement is then to be simultaneously visualized and tacitly recited several times to effectively further cascade empowerment at the PURPOSE stage.

TRUTH

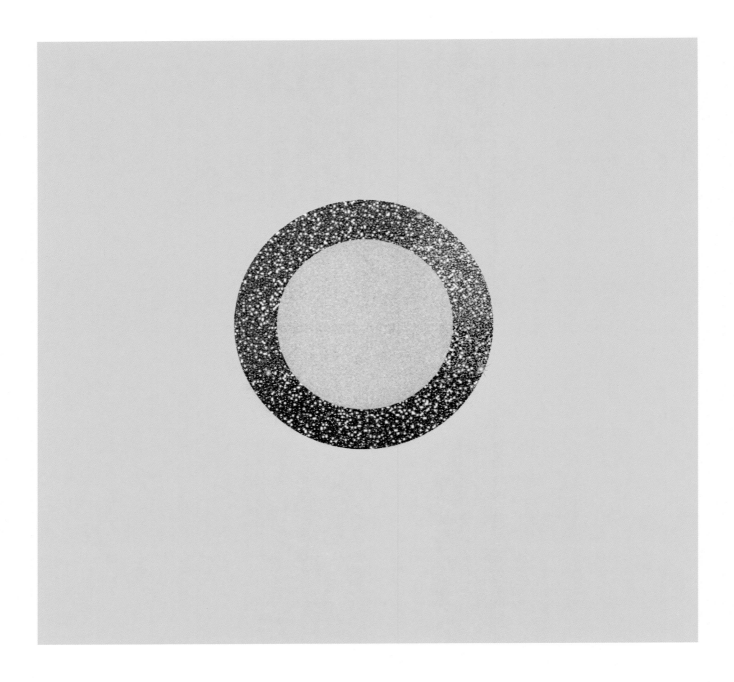

TRUTH SYMBOL PROTOCOL

MANIFEST is the third level of the 'BEST KNOWING JOY' process. TRUTH is the single stage of MANIFEST. The TRUTH stage has been reached as the journey has passed from the cultivation and development of personal traits such as responsibility and integrity through the exercise of Free Will and, subsequently, to the cascading empowerment and application of the TRUST, KNOWING, VISION and PURPOSE stages.

The focus of consciousness during the TRUTH stage as represented by the TRUTH SYMBOL is two-fold. The first being MANIFEST which is a realization experienced and clearly observed resulting directly from activity at the EMPOWERMENT level and which simply becomes MANIFEST. This aspect is represented in the TRUTH SYMBOL by the outer holographic ring.

A second focus, at the expanded Other-consciousness level, is causation where the impact of KNOWING brings cause and effect together resulting in the realization of accomplished TRUTH. The central golden disc of the SYMBOL recognizes the superior level of achievement in the realization of TRUTH accruing to the benefit of the Universal human experience.

The golden disc furthermore represents the JOY of experiencing the MANIFEST realization of the TRUTH. The TRUTH realized through the 'BEST KNOWING JOY' process is always of great importance regardless of magnitude as the achievement adds to the glory of the great Universal TRUTH legacy. We contribute to this legacy in our journey when seeking TRUTH with the clear understanding there is nothing beyond our KNOWING.

MANIFEST

TEMPLATE

TAKEAWAY

AUTHOR'S ADDENDUM

TEMPLATE

'BEST KNOWING JOY' is about the realization of EMPOWERMENT and the successful achievement of PURPOSE, Will and desired outcomes. All manner of MANIFEST and TRUTH will result from the practice and application of the process. The book is much more than the sum of the text, charts, symbols and protocols found in its pages as the action of human consciousness when applied to the fullness of its POTENTIAL is the most powerful force on Earth.

Accepting that we all are heirs to the Legacies, the premise in structuring the book is that everyone having a serious interest in practicing and applying the process should be and will, in fact, be able to do so. Recognizing that the journey is unquestionably ambitious and that consciousness involving mind, body, senses, and psyche is complex, the goal of enabling participation by virtually everyone is challenging but attainable. The rationale for this judgement is as follows:

1. A general awareness of the content and logic of 'BEST KNOWING JOY' is sufficient to acknowledge the goals and related empowerment of the process.

2. The power of using visualization, in general, and SYMBOLS, in particular, is likewise sufficient to communicate information targeted to the various aspects of consciousness.

3. The ability to appropriately calm emotions, select and trigger brain activity levels and effectively focus consciousness is achievable through simple disciplined deep breathing and control of eye motion and eye sight.

4. Activity in accord with the 'BEST KNOWING JOY' process can be successfully performed with intended outcomes by following the instructions and guidance available in THE TEMPLATE presented in the following pages.

The reader is asked to accept the preceding judgement and at this point become personally engaged with the process. To begin, choose to either seek the solution of a worry some problem or identify a heart felt desire to be pursued. Make a specific decision to follow the directions described in THE TEMPLATE. It has been purposely structured to illustrate in a simple yet comprehensive manner the individual steps advancing through the five stages.

In future actual use the process will be found to be highly adaptable to personal and particular situations and, importantly, will invariably involve repetition and recycle within and between stages.

Following THE TEMPLATE pages a listing is given of the procedures, techniques and mechanisms which can be used to intensify and expand the focus of consciousness. At any level of detail or intensity, however, the practice and application of the process will be insightful, interesting, uniquely effective, extremely rewarding and life changing in a very challenging way.

THE TEMPLATE

STAGE/ACTION	BREATH	EYES	SEE	RECITE
TRUST				
	IN	CLOSE	DARKNESS	DARKNESS
	OUT	OPEN	LIGHT	LIGHT
	IN	CLOSE	DARKNESS	PAST TIME
	OUT	OPEN	LIGHT	INSTANT*
	IN	CLOSE	REALITY	PRESENT TRUTH
	OUT	EITHER	SYMBOL	TRUST
KNOWING				
	IN	CLOSE	SPECTRUM**	
	OUT	CLOSE	SYMBOL	KNOWING
	IN	CLOSE	SPECTRUM**	
	OUT	EITHER	SYMBOL	AWARENESS
VISION				
	IN	EITHER	SYMBOL	VISION
	OUT	CLOSE	GOLD RING	
	IN	CLOSE	WHITE DISC	ENVISION
	OUT	CLOSE	DESIRE*	DESIRE
	IN	CLOSE	OUTCOME*	OUTCOME
	OUT	EITHER	SYMBOL	WILL

PURPOSE

	IN	CLOSE	HOLOGRAM**	PURPOSE
	OUT	CLOSE	SYMBOL	EMPOWERMENT
	IN	CLOSE	FOCUS/SHARE*	POTENTIAL
	OUT	EITHER	BE BEST	WE ARE

STAGE/ACTION	BREATH	EYES	SEE	RECITE

TRUTH

	IN	CLOSE	SYMBOL	MANIFEST
	OUT	CLOSE	GOLD DISC	TRUTH
	IN	CLOSE	WILL#	KNOWING
	OUT	CLOSE	MAGNITUDE#	KNOWING
	IN	EITHER	REALIZATION	KNOWING#
	OUT	EITHER	JOY	KNOWING#

KEY

☐	*	SENSE/VISUALIZE SUBJECT/ACTIVITY
☐	**	SEE SYMBOL...OR...CREATE SPECTRUM IMAGE
☐	#	SENSE/EXPERIENCE CAUSATION

TEMPLATE (CONTINUED)

Having gone through THE TEMPLATE exercise it will be evident there are a number of procedures, mechanisms and techniques that are used to focus consciousness. That this is necessary is easily understood considering the multitude of facts, the science and logic and the various elements of consciousness which are involved in the process. The use of SYMBOLS in this regard has been thoroughly described in the previous PROTOCOL section. The following is a listing of other means and related functionality that have been used either separately or in connection with SYMBOLS:

Relaxation response	Calming emotions
Release	Disowning mechanism
Sight switch	Light/dark contrast
Imaging	Image communication
Visualization	Imaging realization
Envisioning	Distortion free visualization
Eye motion	Consciousness detail focusing
Sensing	Bodily/emotional reaction and response
Definition	Knowledge/understanding aid
Seen/spoken	Visual/audio word symbol communication
Causation	Cause/effect combining trigger

Repeating THE TEMPLATE exercise with the additional insight and effectiveness related to these experiential mechanisms will be useful in becoming highly successful in the application of the 'BEST KNOWING JOY' process. When properly executed the process will be seen as unique, dynamic, experiential, empowering and rewarding in many ways.

TAKEAWAY

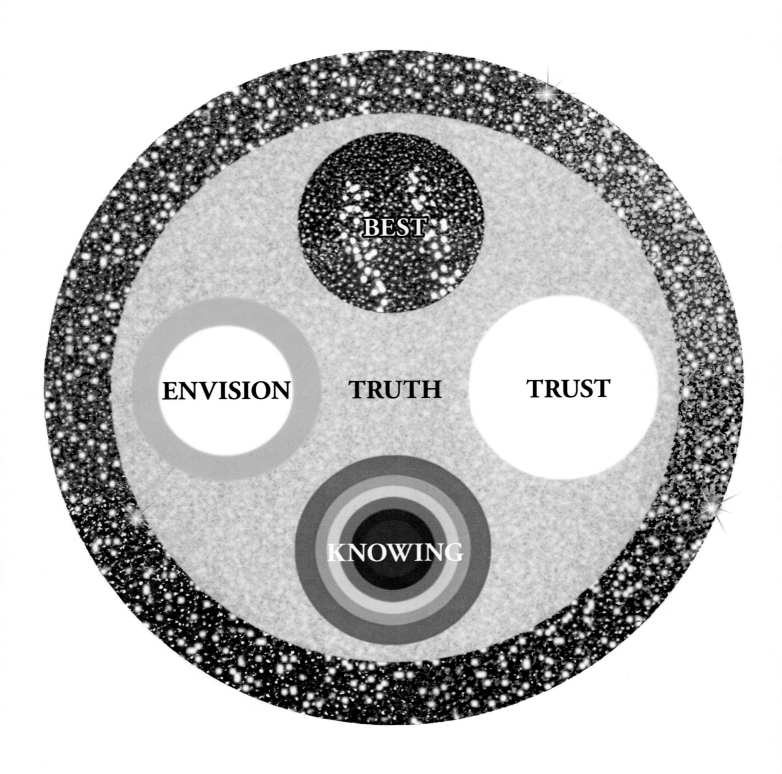

TAKEAWAY

We who are sharing the Human Experience can reasonably make the assertion that we have a claim to legacies arising from all aspects of the creation of the Universe which occurred 13.7 billion years ago. That is an interesting thought which raises questions about what powers are related to the legacies and what part have they played in the shaping of the Human Experience. More specifically, to what extent have these powers been effectively operative as contrasted with being ignored, squandered or adversely used. Further, does a way exist to access these powers upon command for our individual benefit and beyond to that of all mankind.

Curiously, these thoughts merged with my effort to write an insightful book about a series of events occurring during my life that were inexplicable other than by relating them to a single occurrence at an early age. The result of this mingling is significant in that it is a unique approach to using the powers which are our birthright to create the best possible life for us all. The effort has been a challenge.

Having written 'BEST KNOWING JOY' which deals with matters ranging from the Huge Happening to TRUTH in the present INSTANT and having done so over a five year period, the book has been rewritten several times and the TAKEAWAY has been drafted seven or eight times. The challenge has been to produce a TAKEAWAY which works for virtually everyone recognizing that in spite of using several concurrent approaches to convey what I am attempting to share, the challenge remains regarding both substantive content and universal mass acceptance.

There is a solution and it is simple. Once a person, anyone, recognizes that having the desire and making the Free Will decision to make more of their lives the journey and the process can begin. The 'BEST KNOWING JOY' SYMBOL as the vehicle in conjunction with the following comments will create the impact on an individual's consciousness that will anchor all future activities related to the process regardless of the practitioner or the level of detail, simplicity or complexity involved:

TRUST………..Control TIME by focus on the reality of the INSTANT.

KNOWING….Gain Awareness of LEGACIES through focus of consciousness.

VISION……..Truthfulness enables envisioning of Will and desires.

PURPOSE…..EMPOWERMENT cascading to BEST of POTENTIAL.

TRUTH……..Causation and MANIFEST of Will and desires.

Having once read 'BEST KNOWING JOY' and having an understanding of the power and integrity of all of the aspects of the journey, there can be a KNOWING that this TAKEAWAY SYMBOL will serve as an inspired image and solid basis for virtually everyone from which to launch pursuit of self-empowerment, applications related to desired outcomes and the sharing of activities with Others.

AUTHOR'S ADDENDUM

'BEST KNOWING JOY' has been written to significantly change the world for the BEST. In closing, the following comments relate to the text of AUTHOR'S COMMENT and the AUTHOR'S bold initial assertions.

Merely scanning "BEST KNOWING JOY' will change one's life.

Awareness of the legacies and process is itself empowering.

Reading BEST KNOWING JOY' changes one's life for the best.

***Controlling TIME and pursuing TRUTH are obviously
key factors to a successful meaningful life.***

Universal application of the BEST KNOWING JOY' process
will significantly change the world for the best.

***The process empowers from TRUST through PURPOSE and POTENTIAL leading
to the MANIFEST of TRUTH and the experience of FREEDOM and JOY.***

The expectation is that life changing difference on an extensive scale will be realized. The impact on individuals moving from release of negativity through the cascading of EMPOWERMENT to MANIFEST of TRUTH will be significant. Widespread practice of 'BEST KNOWING JOY' will result in societal change with the Universality of PURPOSE and unleashing of unbounded human POTENTIAL. Most importantly, the advent of Universal FREEDOM and TRUTH will be testimony that the Human Experience will continue to benefit from and contribute significantly to the LIGHT and TRUTH legacies.

APPENDIX

KNOWING PVI CURE

STAGE	ACTIVITY	OUTCOME
CONDITION ARISES	SEVERE HEART PALPITATION	ARRHYTHMIA
LIFE THREAT	WILL TOTAL WELLNESS	SEEK 100% CURE
TRUST	MD#1 PRESCRIPTION	DRUGS REJECTED
	MD#2 PRESCRIPTION	PACEMAKER REJECTED
KNOWING	MD#2 DIAGNOSIS	ATRIAL FIBRILLATION
	MD#3 RECOMMENDATION	MD#4 SPECIALIST
VISION	MD#4 CONSULTATION	EXPECT 100% CURE MAJOR SURGICAL RISK
PURPOSE	PULMINARY VEIN ISOLATION DECISION	BE BEST THAT WE ARE
TRUTH	MD#4 SPECIALIST	100% CURE
	PVI SURGERY	TOTAL WELLNESS

KNOWING PVI CURE

In the Introduction it was stated that an event occurring when I was a youngster gave rise to a succession of life changing events. To be slightly more specific, confidently declaring a PURPOSE of magnitude for my life and having absolute certainty that it would be successfully achieved was the initiating event. The PURPOSE involved both achieving a significant long term goal as well as being personally successful in specific ways related to the goal throughout my lifetime. Clearly, by any measure of one and all, both PURPOSE and TRUTH were totally successfully realized.

PURPOSE and TRUTH in our context is not only an idea or ideal driven activity but also includes successful realization, that is, the MANIFEST of PURPOSE and Will. Moreover, there is a focused consciousness and intense effort involved to the extent that our POTENTIAL and, most likely, that of Others is shared and becomes integral to our pursuit of PURPOSE.

In keeping with a legacy having an INTENTION to extend the power and scope of consciousness, we are capable of and presented with opportunities to empower and transfer well-being to Others sharing the Human Experience. These should be understood to be an inherent and integral responsibility associated with activity at the PURPOSE stage.

This latter point is illustrated by a vivid example of the 'BEST KNOWING JOY' process particularly illustrating the transfer of empowerment and the sharing of well-being consciousness as depicted where the PURPOSE of achieving a cure for an abnormal heart condition called atrial fibrillation was being sought. Following an iterative process the successful achievement of curative surgery and recovery was accomplished.

Other-consciousness and the empowerment and POTENTIAL of Others is involved in that at each stage in the process the unknowable and unexpected occurred enabling the pursuit of a successful cure to advance. Each stage TRUST through PURPOSE and, subsequently, TRUTH occurred in this, my wife's actual experience, which clearly MANIFEST a very highly successful, if unlikely, realization of magnitude, namely, a complete cure.

'BEST KNOWING JOY' ALTERNATE TECHNIQUES

STRATEGIC	*TRUST*	*KNOWING*	*VISION*	*PURPOSE*	*TRUTH*
TACTICAL	CONTROL TIME	ELEVATE CONSCIOUSNESS	ENVISION	BE BEST	CAUSATION
ANALYTICAL	INSTANT	KNOWING, OTHER CONSCIOUSNESS	PURPOSE, WILL OTHERS	ATTAINMENT SHARING	MANIFEST WILL/OTHERS
LEGACY	LIGHT DISOWN	LEGACIES SCIENCE	TRUTH AWARENESS	UNBOUNDED POTENTIAL	KNOWING MAGNITUDE
EXPERIENTIAL	REALITY TRUST	UNDERSTANDING CERTAINTY	VIEW, DESIRES SHARING	EMPOWERMENT	REALIZATION JOY
SYMBOLIC	WHITE LIGHT	LIGHT SPECTRUM	LEGACY SPHERE	HOLOGRAM	GOLD LIGHT

'BEST KNOWING JOY' ALTERNATIVE TECHNIQUES

The 'BEST KNOWING JOY' process will be adopted, practiced and applied by many resulting in wide spread application. Consequently, the process to be successful in bringing MANIFEST TRUTH to the masses will ultimately result in a wide variety of approaches to the practice.. Viewing the chart, it is can be seen that depending on circumstances, the resources available and the abilities of the practitioner there are at least six distinct approaches to application extending from strategic to symbolic. In actual practice combinations of the various approaches would often likely be used. Moreover, it is likely that Symbols be used to greatly facilitate practice with whichever approach is employed. No doubt exists that widespread practice and successful application will be realized.

KEY DEFINITIONS

BIRTH RIGHT	Native right or privilege
CAUSATION	The relationship of cause and effect: the act or process of causing
CAUSE	The POWER of efficient agent of producing any thing or event
CONSCIOUSNESS	POWER of self-knowledge
DISOWN	To refuse of acknowledge
ELEVATE	To raise in rank, status, position
EMPOWERMENT	To enable: delegate authority to
ENVISION	To see or foresee in the imagination
EXPERIENCE	Something undergone
FREE WILL	POWER of self-determination
HERITAGE	Any condition which is allotted or handed down to one
HOLOGRAM	Photo containing a three dimensional image made by using laser light to produce the interference pattern of light waves
IMAGINATION	The picturing power or act of the mind: a mental image
INFLUENCE	To act upon physically, affect the nature or condition of: POWER arising from social, financial, moral or similar authority: POWER of providing an effect by imperceptible means
INTEGRITY	Completeness: unimpaired state
JOY	An expression or manifestation of happiness
KNOWING	Possession of reserved knowledge which the person could impart if he chooses
LEGACY	Characteristic derived from an ancestor
LIBERTY	POWER of voluntary choice
MAGNITUDE	Great size or extent: importance
MANIFEST	To make plain to sight or understanding: reveal, display.
OTHERS	Any or all involved with the principal
OTHER-CONSCIOUSNESS	State of expanded consciousness resulting from realization of empowerment derived from LIGHT and TRUTH legacies
PERCEPTION	Knowledge through senses of properties of external world
POTENTIAL	Indicating possibility or POWER

POWER	The property of a substance or being that is manifested in effort or action and by virtue of which that substance or being produces change, moral or physical
PURPOSE	The idea or ideal kept before the mind as an end of effort or action
REALIZATION	The act of converting into fact
RESPONSIBILITY	State of being accountable
SYMBOL	Something chosen to represent because of resemblance
TRUST	Confidence: the state of one who has received an important charge: a confidence in the reliability of persons of things without careful investigation
TRUTH	Conforming to fact or reality
UNDO	To cause to be as if never done
VISION	Ability to anticipate and make provision for future events
VISUALIZATION	To form a mental image: picture in the mind
WILL	The POWER of conscious, deliberate action

LEGACIES AND FOCUS AIDS

The 'BEST KNOWING JOY' process creates and cascades EMPOWERMENT through the focus of consciousness based on LIGHT and TRUTH legacies. The practice and application involves the human psyche extending from the mind through to bodily senses.

Although the words of the text and SYMBOLS directly and specifically related to the legacies are the primary vehicles for communicating knowledge and the understanding and application of the PROCESS and PROTOCOL, other means as listed in the TEMPLATE pages of the MANIFEST section can and will be used. These other and related alternative means will extend the range of visualization and visual and audio imaging as well as create opportunities to employ tactile sensing. Even extra-sensory possibilities may develop.

The scope of the legacies and the POTENTIAL related to the breadth of consciousness suggest a wide range of creative and tangible possibilities for enhancing the experience of effectively focusing consciousness.

REFERENCES

The author of 'BEST KNOWING JOY' has had an interest in area of consciousness for nearly seven decades. The content of shelves of books, audio tapes, DVDs and magazines concerning all aspects of consciousness have provided a great deal to think about, experiment with and practice and develop over that period. Combining that experience with my interest in various fields of science have created the base from which the attempt has been made to understand the events in my life in the most basic terms. The writing of the book has taken four years. I acknowledge and am thankful for all the knowledge gained from sources and references too numerous to mention. My sincere hope is that my insight into the TRUTH in my life does justice to the efforts of all who have been my mentors.

Printed in the United States
By Bookmasters